MW01707746

REBRAND

How to overcome adversity and create the life you desire

Andrew Bawa

Copyright © 2020 by Andrew Bawa.

All rights reserved. No part of this publication may be reproduced, distributed or transmitted in any form or by any means, including photocopying, recording, or other electronic or mechanical methods, without the prior written permission of the Author/Publisher, except in the case of brief quotations embodied in critical reviews and certain other noncommercial uses permitted by copyright law.

For permission requests, write to the author/publisher, addressed "Attention: Permissions Coordinator," at the address below:

1308 Chevrier Blvd,
Winnipeg, MB R3T 1Y3
pastorbawa@gmail.com

Ordering Information:

Quantity sales. Special discounts are available on quantity purchases by corporations, associations, and others.

For details, contact the "Special Sales Department" at the address above.

REBRAND/Andrew Bawa. —1st ed.

ISBN: 978-1-988497-09-9

Dedication

My beautiful wife, Yenkat. Your strength and resilience in bouncing back from the enemy's attack is awe-inspiring. Through it all, you have been an epitome of elegance and grace. I am excited to see what the future holds.

Table of Contents

ACKNOWLEDGMENTS

I would like to thank my family for their love and support. My wife, Yenkat, and my daughters, Elswidih and Elnessa. Thank you for being patient with me, supporting me and cheering me on.

I would also like to appreciate Theresa Simba and the team that worked tirelessly to make this project a success.

INTRODUCTION

From time memorial, man has been evolving. There are so many theories of the evolution of man; Some people believe in the Darwinian theory, while others believe that there is a creator who brought the world to life. No matter where you stand, you cannot deny that the world is changing, and that man is evolving. Some years ago we used analogue phones, and now, about 20 years later, we have evolved to using smartphones. Even smartphones are evolving by expanding their use and being multifunctional. Companies are merging together to create more improved products and services so that they can keep up in this ever changing market or they risk being extinct.

Convenience is at the forefront of the current market; For example, people do not need to travel to a central location anymore in order to have meetings. Services like zoom or google hangouts have been created for that. People no longer need to go to the grocery stores, they can easily order their groceries online and have them delivered to their homes. Just a few years ago, these services did not exist.

In all of this, we learn that we cannot use yesterday's methods to conquer tomorrow's victories. You must be able to come out of the shallowness of your current position and be on the vanguard of history making ventures if you want to remain relevant.

In light of all of this, I want to look at what is happening in the world and compare it to a very peculiar story of a lady in the Bible. There are only 2 books of the Bible that are named after women; Ruth and Esther. In this book, we will study the story of Ruth.

I was intrigued by Ruth's story, of how this lady from the cursed tribe of Moab completely changed the trajectory of her life. She was able to move to a different country where she did not know the language or culture but still managed to make something out of her life. Ruth was not only able to evolve in her generation but also in a land where she was considered cursed.

What did she do to get there? How did she get into the nation of Israel and the city of Bethlehem and become one of the most influential women in the city? How did she end up marrying one of the wealthiest men in the city? How was she able to come to a different city after losing everything and still evolve and emerge as a force to be reckoned with?

Psalms 22:30 says, "A seed shall serve him; it shall be accounted to the Lord for a generation". Ruth served the Lord in her generation. She did what she needed to do, and she was so relevant and revelatory that she became the great grandmother of Jesus.

Many believers rely so much on prayer, but they forget principles. Prayer is so vital, but it has to be coupled with following biblical principles in order for you to make a difference. In this book, we will examine eight principles that we can draw from Ruth.

I believe that this book will be a blessing to you. The whole premise is how to rebrand yourself. In this ever changing world of technology and social media, how do you remain relevant and revelatory? Relevant to deal with the present situation in our generation and revelatory to have an impact in the future, while also not denying our experiences.

As we enter a new decade, I look forward to seeing you rebranding yourself so that you will become sought after. You have something to offer, no one is a non-entity. You are created for a purpose; you have an assignment, a product, a mission and there is a group of people waiting with eager expectation to receive what you carry.

1

CRISIS

You may hear the word "brand" every so often. With the rise of entrepreneurship, especially online in this era of social media, branding is very important. I can bet the things that come to mind when you think of branding are colours, logos, websites and other such things. But experts tell us that although these things are important, they aren't necessarily what attracts customers or consumers to a certain brand or product. What attracts them to it is what they believe about a brand or how a brand makes them feel.

Martin Roll says that the ultimate goal in business is to create a perception of your company, its products and services that are valuable, meaningful and most importantly, different from competitors.

I would say that rebranding is re-introducing who you are to your customers or clients. It is creating a new identity that will make you stand out in the marketplace. In order to properly represent who you are to others, you have to understand that identity for yourself. You have to know your brand and believe in it before you can change anyone else's perception or convince anyone to believe in you.

Whether or not you brand yourself is, in itself, a brand. Your promise (and delivery) to your customers is your brand.

Knowing who you are is the most important thing you can do to rebrand yourself. You have to believe in your brand before you can change anyone else's perception of it.

YOU ARE A BRAND

Now, you could easily argue that branding only applies to entrepreneurs or only those who are in the business world. But I would like to challenge that idea and suggest to you that who you are or who you present yourself to be is also a brand.

Consider these simple scenarios; How often have you met someone for the first time and formed an opinion about them within the first few minutes? How they present themselves helps you form an opinion about who they are.

We are often told that first impressions matter, and in response to that, we make sure that we dress well, speak eloquently and present ourselves at our possible best when going for a job interview. We do everything in our power to create a perception to the hiring manager or interviewer that we are the exceptional talent that they are looking for.

The lesson on first impressions also overflows to the dating and relationship world. When we meet or are pursuing someone for the first time, we make sure they see and experience the best version of us. We take our time to convince them and build trust that we are the best choice for them.

In both scenarios, we see that we are branding ourselves so that our client (the hiring manager and romantic interest) are interested in the product we are offering (ourselves).

Now that we have established that we are also a brand, it is important that we know our brand identity so that we may be able to convey or represent ourselves appropriately.

WHAT IS YOUR BRAND IDENTITY?

Just like a business's brand identity is what makes them stand out from the crowd, your personal identity is what makes you uniquely you.

> "**Personal identity** is the concept you develop about yourself that evolves over the course of your life. This may include aspects of your life that you

have no control over, such as where you grew up or the colour of your skin, as well as the choices you make in life, such as how you spend your time and what you believe. You demonstrate portions of your personal identity outwardly through what you wear and how you interact with other people. You may also keep some elements of your personal identity to yourself, even when these parts of yourself are very important."

— Christina Serva.

When God created us, He gave us an identity and a purpose. Over the course of our lives, we misconstrue that God-given identity because of our life choices or circumstances that are beyond our control.

We get so cluttered by the things that have happened to us or that we have experienced and we start portraying ourselves according to those circumstances. Even the writers of the Bible have, in various settings, referred to people according to their situation. Multiple examples come to mind; "the woman with the issue of blood", "the widow of Zarephath", "blind Bartimaeus" and so on and so forth.

Every day we see a number of people struggling with their identities and with who they are. There are many drowning under the weight of the labels that have been given to them by society or even labels that they have given to themselves.

The only way to be able to know who you are is to know who your maker is.

It is of paramount importance that you go back to the beginning and discover who you are - discover what God had intended for you from the very beginning, discover your true and unique identity.

NEW CREATION REALITIES

This means that anyone who belongs to Christ has become a new person. The old life is gone; a new life has begun!

2 Corinthians 5:17

The moment you surrender your life to Jesus, you become a completely new person. I like to use Paul as an example when speaking of becoming a new creation.

Before he became a believer, Apostle Paul (who was known as Saul at that time) went around different places to murder believers. He was a threat to the church at that time, people were terrified of him. But after he had an encounter on his way to Damascus, everything changed.

Not only did his name change, his mission and purpose turned around completely. Instead of going around and destroying the church, he became an apostle of the church and went ahead to write a huge chunk of the New Testament. All the old things had passed away, Paul became new.

This is exactly what happens to anyone who has surrendered to Christ as their Lord and personal Saviour. Their slate is wiped clean. You are no longer held responsible for anything you had done before then. You are no longer the person you used to be. Everything becomes new.

As a new creation, you take on a new identity. You become exactly who God created you to be. You are now called and chosen by God. He gives you a new vision, mission and purpose. You become more than just a number, you carry a mandate with you. This is why the bible calls you the salt of the earth; you are called to add value to the world and to shine a light.

As a new creation, it is of utmost importance that you consistently renew your mind. When you get saved, your spirit is saved but your mind and your old way of thinking remains the same. That is why you need to renew your mind daily. You have spent your entire life so far thinking a certain way, so it will take renewing your mind to change the way you think.

You need to study the characteristics of the new creation, study who God says you are, study what God says about you and what He has promised you. This takes time but the more you renew your mind, the more the labels society has placed on you start to fall off. Even the way you see yourself changes. You are slowly being renewed to become who God wants you to be.

The more you discover who you are in Christ, the more confident and sure you get. People's opinions stop mattering when you know what the King of Kings says about you. Your purpose becomes clearer - you become more focused than ever before.

As you live in this new reality, you will eventually stop trying to prove yourself to others and you will just be who you are - a light. Light does not struggle with darkness. It provides illumination, clarity and direction. You are light and you will shine.

You are light and you will shine. You are not meant to be caged. You are called for a global mission. Your life is for impact. So acknowledge your calling, be the best version of yourself, reset and reprogram your mind.

The process of changing completely may seem slow but be patient with yourself. Remember that good things take time. As you continue to discover who you are and what you stand for, you are building your brand. This is how a brand is built, one step at a time, and at the end you will have reason to celebrate what you have built.

THE CRISIS

Most of us have heard the story of Ruth, the young Moabite who married into a Jewish family and became one of the notable women in the lineage of Jesus.

Even though her story has a happy ending, it did not start that way. At some point in her life, Ruth was happily married to her Jewish husband and lived with her family in Moab. But slowly, things began to change for the worse. Ruth lost her husband and her brother in law. Before long, her happy family was no longer the same. Death struck and made her a widow.

Just like Ruth, there are times in our lives where adversity strikes and our lives are changed as a result of it. Sometimes we recover quickly while other times a lot of inner work has to be done before we are able to recover. Adversity can change your brand identity. Look at Ruth, death struck and she suddenly had to transition from being a young bride to a widow.

Life has a way of throwing you some unexpected curveballs. If you are well equipped to handle said curveballs you will be better positioned to recover and come back even stronger. Otherwise, you can be stuck in negative cycles of past pain and hurt which can determine the course of the rest of your life.

In the following chapters, we will discuss how Ruth, a foreigner, was able to completely turn her life around by using the power of rebranding. This is why I wrote this book; I want you to know that there is no adversity you can not recover from - with the right tools, you can bounce back and create the life you desire. Your best days are still ahead of you.

2

CHANGE

In the book of Ruth, chapter 1 to 4, we see the story of Ruth, a young Moabite woman who was widowed at an early age. She lived in Moab with her mother-in-law, Naomi and her sister-in-law, Orpah.

Naomi was an Israelite who moved to Moab with her husband and two sons. After losing her husband and children, Naomi decided to go back to her homeland, Judah.

As the story goes, her daughters-in-law set out with her but only Ruth actually followed through with her decision to go back with Naomi to Judah.

"Look," said Naomi, "your sister-in-law is going back to her people and her gods. Go back with her." But Ruth replied, "Don't urge me to leave you or to turn back from you. Where you go I will go, and where you stay I will stay. Your people will be my people and your God, my God.

Ruth 1:15-16

Change is difficult, especially when one is already set in their ways. Orpah had never been to Judah, Moab was all she knew. Leaving Moab would mean starting over in a completely strange place, away from all she knew, and all that was near and dear to her. It's easy to point fingers at Orpah for not going all the way with Naomi, but when you really think about it, most of us are like her - resistive to change.

Ruth, on the other hand, embraced the change. Ruth and Orpah had already gone through some traumatic changes so far. They had lost their husbands and were on the verge of losing their mother-in-law. Logically, it made sense for Orpah to want to embrace the familiar. But we see that after she left, she was never spoken of again.

In the process of rebranding, it is easy to lose your relevance if you do not embrace change no matter how difficult it may be. For example, look at the rise of technology right now. Everything is becoming more tech based. People are losing jobs as they are being replaced by machines. Stores are shutting down as they are being replaced by online shopping. Those who did not jump on the change wagon when it first began, are currently suffering the consequences of resisting change. The world is changing fast and we have to keep up with it. Be willing to change your perspective; the way you see things or the way you do things. It is important to be flexible.

In all essentials, let there be unity. In non-essentials let there be liberty. In all things, let there be charity. - St Augustine of Hippo

As important as change is, do not change your core. Your core is the inner sense of who you are, it is your purpose. You can change your behaviour, which is the way you relate or respond. You can also change your character, which comes as a result of your environment.

A lot of people grow up believing or hearing that they cannot achieve certain things or go beyond a certain level in their life. This is as a result of the environment they grew up in: what they've heard, what they've seen or what they've been told is the norm. Ruth was willing to change her environment, and that eventually changed her life.

You can also change your awareness. Changing your awareness means that you see beyond the reality of your circumstances in that moment. For example, let's say you're currently completely broke, instead of dwelling on what is at that moment and accepting it as the final verdict of your life, open your mind up to another reality - the reality of wealth. Dwell on that. Feed your awareness with what could be. Your reality can not change if you're unaware of the possibilities of all you could become.

HOW DO YOU CHANGE?

Acknowledge your current state

If you're looking to, let's say, get rid of debt or lose some weight, the first step you'll take is take stock of where you currently are. If it's debt, you'll need to know exactly how much you owe and what habits brought you to that position. With weight loss it's the same thing, you acknowledge where you currently are and point out the behaviours that brought you to that point. Before you make any changes, it is of paramount importance that you acknowledge your current state.

To acknowledge is to recognise. Take a real long look at your life and your circumstances. Recognise who you currently are and the state of your life at the moment. Recognise the part that you played to be where you are, and even the part that was not your fault. In order to change your life, it is imperative that you know who you truly are.

Challenge that state

Set goals:

A lot of people talk about setting goals but very few speak about how to set goals the right way. I will delve a little deeper on how to set goals for yourself to get to where you want to be.

You can ask yourself these simple questions before you start your goal-setting process: Where do you want to go? How are you going to get there? Do you have a plan? These questions create the entire framework for setting goals. The goal-setting process is a simple yet powerful process.

To start off, have a vision for yourself. This comes when you answer the first question which is, where do you want to go? It is best to start with the big picture. Visualise where you want to be in the next 5, 10 or even 15 years. What do you see? Write down the big picture goals for yourself. Some people even prefer to create a vision board so that they can clearly see what they want for themselves.

After having your big picture or vision, answer the second question; how are you going to get there? In this second step, what you need to do is to break down your big picture goal into smaller chunks that you can work with. For example if your big picture goal is to save an extra $30,000 in the next 3 years. Your smaller goal can be increasing your income by $10,000 in the next 12 months.

The final question to answer is where you get down to the nitty gritty. Make a plan. How are you going to increase your income in the next 12 months? This is where you write down the how. From the example above, the plan could be to get a second job or start a small business. Whatever your goal is, have actionable steps that you can take in order to achieve that goal.

The final step would be to follow through. There is no point writing down goals if you have no plans to follow through with them. This is why it is important that you set SMART goals. SMART is an acronym for Specific, Measurable, Achievable, Realistic and Timely.

Break the limiting beliefs

Every change starts in the mind before it manifests in the physical. You have to decide that you really want to change an area in your life. It will be difficult because most times you are already set in your ways. You'll have to change patterns that you have built over long periods of time. You'll want to quit but you will have to make the necessary sacrifices in order to change. Because it is difficult, it is important that you break of the thoughts that limit you. And you can do this by daily renewing your mind (Romans 12:2). The mindset that got you to where you are was not built in a day, therefore, renewing your mind is a daily exercise.

A majority of us are limited by fear. The fear of failure, fear of success and the fear of the unfamiliar are at the root of most limiting beliefs. The reality is, a number of things we are afraid of are based on a lie. A good way to overcome limiting beliefs is to discover this lie and counter it with the truth of God's word. This is what it means to renew your mind. It is often a long process that has to be done consistently and intentionally.

In this process of uncovering the lies and replacing them with the truth, be careful of the people or the surroundings you find yourself in. You have a higher affinity to the lies because you have believed them for so long. In order to change, you will need to surround yourself with truth. Watch, talk to and seek people who have overcome the beliefs you are trying to overcome. Surround yourself with those who have done or are doing the things that you want to do but thought were impossible for you to do. Fill your mind with possibilities and positivity. This will encourage you and help you to slowly overcome the limiting beliefs.

Have accountability

Accountability will help you stay on track, especially on the days that you are struggling to stick to your goals. Having someone to keep you accountable is great, but really, accountability starts with you. It is important that you take ownership of your decisions and your actions as you journey towards becoming your best version.

A practical way to be accountable is to have an accountability partner. This is someone who will hold you accountable for your actions as per your mutual agreement. You may both decide to hold each other accountable as you stay on top of your goals, or if you are pursuing a similar goal, you can even make it a healthy competition. This is effective as it gives you a challenge and it also makes implementing change appealing; It is more fun to do it with a friend than to do it alone.

If you prefer to be accountable to yourself, another practical tip is to reward yourself along the journey. Congratulate yourself on how far you have come and encourage yourself to go even further. Seeking feedback from a loved one is also a good way to hold yourself accountable as you see your improvement through their eyes.

In Chapter 2 of the book of Ruth, we see that Ruth and Naomi are now settled in Judah. The Bible says that they had arrived during the harvest season. Ruth was in a foreign land, but even in the midst of all that, Ruth was able to make 3 significant changes.

The first change she made was she adjusted quickly and went to work. Ruth did not sit around and wait for handouts or make excuses based on her current circumstances. She did not wait for the government to give her welfare or a well-meaning individual to support her and Naomi financially. She adjusted quickly and went straight to work so that she and Naomi could support themselves.

The second change Ruth made was her garments. We all know the old adage that how you dress is how you'll be addressed. Well, Ruth came into Bethlehem in her widow's garments. That was her brand. For a whole year, Ruth lived in Bethlehem dressed as a widow and working in Boaz's field during the harvest season. This continued until her mother-in-law, Naomi, told her to change her garments in Ruth 3:3.

Now do as I tell you—take a bath and put on perfume and dress in your nicest clothes. Then go to the threshing floor, but don't let Boaz see you until he has finished eating and drinking.

Ruth 3:3

The third change that Ruth made was that she was able to get out of her comfort zone. The fact she left Moab and followed Naomi to a foreign land, away from everything that was familiar to her, shows that Ruth had left her comfort zone. When she got to Boaz's farm, she got comfortable gleaning behind the workers. In those times, most of the workers were foreigners thus it was easy for Ruth to hang out with people who were foreigners like she was. She had met Boaz before, but after she changed her garments and got out of her comfort zone, she was able to meet Boaz under different circumstances.

Are you willing to change your garments?

Many of us want to go higher and move forward without paying the price of change. Just like blind Bartimaeus, some levels require a change of garments. When Jesus called blind Bartimaeus in Mark 10:50, the first thing that he did was to remove his garments. Many times, our garments define us, enslave us and limit us.

Until we are willing to change, there are some levels of breakthrough that we will not experience.

Dress for success

As vain as this may sound to some people, the way you dress has an impact on your brand. Clothes make a visual statement of how you see yourself and how others will perceive you. Career mentors advise people to dress for the job they want and not the job they have. People are more willing to trust you when you are dressed a certain way. What we wear is definitely an important part of our brand identity.

The way you dress does not only affect the way others see you but also the way you see yourself. Research says that those who dress better feel more confident and more powerful. Their colleagues look to them for answers and for help and there is a sense of heightened respect.

A lot can be said about your brand because of the way you dress. If you are a business owner looking for investors or trying to win more clients, you have a better chance of convincing an investor or client to partner with you when you are dressed right. The way you dress will affect their first impression of you and even their decision to work with you. Dressing well brings you the right kind of attention and also increases productivity.

A disclaimer I would like to give here is that dressing well does not mean going into debt to buy designer clothes. It simply means you wear decent clothing that is neat, clean, properly ironed and appropriate for the occasion.

3

CONNECTION

In this age of the internet and social media, connection has been easier and faster than it has ever been. If we are looking for a certain product or information, we can easily find it by going on google. Likewise, if one is looking for a job, they are advised to brush up their LinkedIn accounts or go through their contacts so that they may get referrals. In more ways than one, we see the importance of connection and how it can impact our lives.

As the saying goes, there are no strong men anywhere, there are only helped men. If you are going to succeed in life, it is important to make good connections. Connections are the relationships that we have.

"Who you follow determines what follows you,"

Your relationships will determine how far you go in life. Your relationships can either make you or break you. In the story of Ruth, we see that Ruth was able to get to Boaz because of her relationship with Naomi. But in this day and age, many people - especially young people, trample on their Naomi in the process of trying to get to their Boaz without knowing that Naomi can be the help you need to get to Boaz.

We see from chapter 2 that Naomi already knew that Ruth was going to Boaz's field. She already knew that Boaz was a close relative and that he would be a candidate to be Ruth's husband. But Naomi did not introduce or even mention that concept to Ruth. Naomi had to observe Ruth, she had to test her character.

Naomi already knew the Jewish laws and traditions, she knew that a close relative was required to make an honest woman out of Ruth. But she did not bring that up to Ruth right away.

If Ruth had severed ties with Naomi, she would have missed out on her blessing. We can clearly see that Ruth's relationship with Naomi played a huge part in the outcome of her story.

The relationships you build and maintain throughout the course of your life will determine how far you will go. There are a number of people who receive access or opportunities as a result of the people they know. Sometimes, it is not about your skills or qualifications, there are people that have been placed in your life who will lead you to where you want to go.

It has been said that you cannot pay your way to the top but you can relate your way to the top. Look around you, who do you have? What kind of relationships are you building with your peers? How often do you go for team or networking events? Are you likable or approachable? Can you hold a conversation or do you isolate yourself from others?

These are important questions that you should ask as you are working on rebranding yourself. I would advise that you be completely honest in this self-evaluation process so that you can know where you are and work out a solution to make positive changes.

As you do this self-evaluation, it is also a great time to evaluate the relationships that you currently have. What kind of people do you surround yourself with? Have you not heard that you are the sum total of the people that you hang around? Your network will determine your net worth.

There are four levels of relationships that you should know:

The crowd

This is the outside layer of your relationships. These are the people that are around you but not necessarily close to you or part of your communities. These are the people you meet every day, as you drive or take the bus or go to the mall.

The community

These are the people who share your values. It is possible to have more than one community of people around you. It may be people from your church, work or school. If you are involved in one or more things in your life, you may have a community of people that you associate with there.

The connected

These are your acquaintances. They may be your colleagues at work, your classmates in school, or the members of your church. You know them personally even though you may not be that close.

The committed

These are your people. They are your friends. These are the people who are with you and for you all the way. Within this group of people, you will have your core. The core is the inner circle - they are your closest. There are, usually, not more than 3 people in your core. The core are your confidants, these are the people you are accountable to.

When we take a good look at the life of Jesus, we can see that He also had these four levels of relationships. It is clear that the 12 disciples were 'The Committed', and within the committed, Jesus had the core; Peter, James and John. These are the ones he took to his most intimate moments.

So, as you evaluate the relationships in your life, keep these things in perspective. Use wisdom in your conversations and in your dealings. For example, you can't share with the crowd the things that are meant for your core. The level of trust you have in your relationships is different with each group of people.

Do not be so deceived and misled! Evil companionships (communion, associations) corrupt and deprave good manners and morals and character.

1 Corinthians 15:33

MENTORS AND ADVISORS

In speaking of relationships, it is of paramount importance that we speak of the people you allow to advise you or pour into you.

I mentioned earlier in the chapter that if Ruth had no regard for Naomi, she would not have ended up as Boaz's wife. Naomi mentored her, gave her handholding, and her life was changed forever.

Sometimes many people, especially young people, tend to ignore the advice of those who have gone before them. Granted that you should always have discernment about the advice that you receive, but do not completely ignore those who have gone before you. Especially when you know that these people care about you and want the best for you.

It is possible to have different mentors for different areas of your life. Mentorship is not about age; when a person knows more than you know about a certain subject that you need, they can potentially mentor you in that area. They don't necessarily have to be older than you. For instance, one of my daughters mentors me when it comes to finances. If I were to consider her age I would miss out on the wealth of wisdom that she has to offer.

God did not design man to live by themselves. Just as He said in Genesis 2:18 that it is not good for a man to be alone. No man is an island, we all need each other. Locate the people that you can lean on and learn from.

In 1 Kings 12, we see King Solomon's son, Rehoboam, needing direction on a decision he had to make. In verse 6, he consulted the older men who stood before Solomon while he was yet alive and asked them for advice. The older men advised him but verse 8 says that he forsook the counsel that these men gave him and instead, he consulted his peers - the people who grew up with him.

Listen, do not always go with the decision that tickles your fancy. Sometimes, what is good for you may not feel good at the moment or may not be the advice that you want to hear at that time but go with it anyway, especially when you know that it's good for you.

Rehoboam went with the advice from his peers and as a result, he lost a portion of the kingdom that he was supposed to rule over.

Be mindful of the people that you allow to pour into you or speak over your life. You do not want to lose your kingdom just because you listened to the wrong advice. Prayerfully consider your options every time, submit every advice or decision to God and He will direct your path.

PARASITIC RELATIONSHIPS

In the same way, as you build your relationships, it is vital that you are genuine and authentic. Do not try to connect with people because you want to get something from them. Do not be parasitic. Relationships are built and strengthened based on trust, and it takes some time to build trust. It is very easy for people to notice when you're only trying to connect because you want something. That is the fastest way to lose a relationship and also ruin your reputation.

With regard to mentors, most people make a mistake because they want to be takers instead of being servants. Before a person can completely pour into you and teach what they know, you have to build a relationship with them.

It has been said that we find ourselves when we lose ourselves in the service of others. Let's take a look at Elijah and Elisha's relationship; for many years Elisha served Elijah diligently without expecting anything in return. There was no platform, no pay, nothing of material value that he could gain from this relationship. But eventually we see that Elijah's mantle was transferred to Elisha. Elisha ended up doing twice as many miracles than his mentor. Service was what caused Elisha to discover and work in the true calling of his life.

The Bible tells us that before Elisha started serving Elijah, he was a successful businessman, he had 6 employees under him. When God called him, he left all of that to serve Elijah. He served under him for 20 years. It did not seem like he got anything in return.

Before Elijah was taken up to heaven, Elisha expressed his desire of getting a double portion of his anointing. In 2 Kings 2:11, when Elijah was being taken up by the chariot of fire, Elisha was clearly distressed. He wasn't there for the double portion anointing, he was there because he had built a relationship with Elijah. His attention was not on the mantle, his attention was on the man.

When God saw that Elisha had a heart for his master as opposed to only wanting a double portion of his anointing, God released that mantle to him.

We should all learn from Elisha to serve and build a relationship without any hidden agenda. Do not try to build a relationship with someone so that you can take, take and take from them. Serve them. Let the connection be mutually beneficial. Be sincere and genuine in your dealings and God will honour you.

4

CHARACTER

We have already established that connections are important. But even more important is your character. Character would determine whether you will be able to sustain a relationship or not.

There is an African proverb that says that character is like pregnancy, it cannot be hidden. You can try to put up a facade for someone, and that may be successful for a while but it will not last very long. The true you will always come out.

Character refers to the particular and distinctive qualities of a person. It has been said that good character is the most important attribute to living a successful and worthy life. Character is who you are. This is what your reputation will be based on.

It was character that made Naomi eventually introduce Ruth to Boaz. Naomi already knew the Jewish traditions. She was well aware that Boaz could eventually marry Ruth but she did not mention it to her initially. It is clear that Ruth already had the connection, but the connection alone was not what got her to Boaz.

Ruth had to be tested and proved. Think about it, would you be comfortable introducing your major connection, or someone you highly respect to another person that you do not trust? I am sure you would not be okay with it. You would know that if that person's character comes to light, it may destroy the relationship you have with that connection.

Naomi had to test Ruth. She had to test her character and make sure that she could be trusted. Now, it is possible that Ruth could pretend when she was with Naomi just to get in her good books. It was completely possible for her to convince Naomi that she was the perfect daughter-in-law when in reality she was not. But like I mentioned earlier, the true her would have been revealed with time.

In marketing, we have been taught countless times that clients do business with people they know, like and trust. If you have a bad character, it is almost impossible for people to like and trust you. Your business and brand will suffer because of it.

People who do business with you or want to interact with your brand will do their due diligence in finding out all there is to know about you. They will do their research. They will ask people who know you have heard of you or those who have done business with you. If these people are wise, they will find out everything they need to know.

If you have poor character and no integrity, they will know. That will sabotage your business or brand. Look at Boaz for example, before he made his decision, he asked around about Ruth. He did his research on her. If Ruth was a bad person with poor character he would have found out. If Ruth was rude or disrespectful to the workers in Boaz's field, he would have found that out too.

Then Boaz asked his foreman, "Who is that young woman over there? Who does she belong to?"

6 And the foreman replied, "She is the young woman from Moab who came back with Naomi. 7 She asked me this morning if she could gather grain behind the harvesters. She has been hard at work ever since, except for a few minutes' rest in the shelter."

Ruth 2:5-7

Your character will always speak on your behalf. You never know who is watching you and trying to find out about you. Boaz had been watching Ruth long before they ended up married. The foreman only had good things to say about her when he was asked. Do you know what people would say about you in your absence? How do you treat others? What is your character?

Charisma may take you to the top, but character will keep you there.

Charisma is not enough. My mentor, John Maxwell, once said to me that his name will open the door for me but it takes character for me to remain there. I equate character to integrity. Integrity is simply who you are when no one is watching. Are you trustworthy? Are you a person of your word? Can we go to the bank with your word?

Surprisingly, most people who have excellent character - are trustworthy, straight forward and stand for the truth, are not usually liked by others. Truth is painful and most people do not want to hear it so they end up disliking everyone who speaks the truth. But regardless of what others think, you must be willing to change your character if you want to change your life.

HOW CAN YOU CHANGE YOUR CHARACTER?

Just like any other change one decides to make, the first step in changing your character is identifying the problem; which in this case is a character flaw. Ask yourself these three questions: What is it that you want to change? What does your ideal finished product look like? How will you get there?

After identifying what the problem is, then you are in a good place to set goals on how to deal with the said problem. Nothing can be done well without a plan. In Chapter 2, we spoke about change more in-depth, and we went through how to set smart goals. The same principles apply in this case as well.

I would also advise that you ask a trusted person or group of people who know you well. Ask them what they think of you, how they see you and what character flaws you should work on. This is also a good way to identify character flaws that could not be easily identified on your own

These trusted few will also be an excellent source of feedback and accountability as you journey towards your desired change. Because they love you, it would be easier to receive correction from them. They can also be the ones to encourage you when you are down and motivate you when you want to give up. They will be your support system and even congratulate you when they start seeing the manifestation of the work you have put in in order to change. A support system is vital in such a process, especially because it is a long process to go through.

Change usually starts in the mind. If you used to think a certain way, in order to change, you'll need to renew your mind and think differently and in a way that is supportive of the change you are making. A good way to renew your mind is to read from people who are where you want to be or who have walked a similar path and have overcome. Reading opens your mind to new realms of possibilities, and when your mind is stretched and changed, you won't be able to go back to the old way of how you used to think. Renewing your mind is a prerequisite to any change in action.

Don't copy the behaviour and customs of this world, but let God transform you into a new person by changing the way you think. Then you will learn to know God's will for you, which is good and pleasing and perfect.

Romans 12:2

It is also important to be aware of the environment you place yourself. , The people who surround you have a great impact on you. The people you associate with affect your brand. Be intentional about surrounding yourself with people who will support you and help you as you challenge yourself to become better. The company you keep will influence you to be better or worse. The bible says that bad company corrupts good character, so again, evaluate the relationships around you..

It is easy to get discouraged, especially when you are trying to do something that is new or different from what you normally do. Your friends may start questioning or laughing at you and cause you to doubt what you do. Apart from outside pressure, it also requires a lot of discipline on your part to change something that has been a part of you for a very long time. So, be patient with yourself in pursuit of this better version of you. Realise that change takes time. It is usually an ongoing process because we don't stop growing.

5

CREATIVITY

Creativity, simply put, is the ability to create. In order to create, we need to be able to apply our thinking faculties. If we want to be successful, we need to be able to think.

For most people, they associate thinking with thinking about their problems, past or what people are talking about. But the truth of the matter is, thinking is what enables our creativity. Creativity is the ability to chart a new path, think outside of the box and make something from what seems like nothing.

When you are in a rut, creativity enables you to figure out how to adjust, how to use the resources that you have and how to find a way out of the situation you find yourself in. creativity is what makes you a trail blazer, travelling the road that isn't usually taken.

In Chapter 3 of the book of Ruth, we see Ruth and Naomi being very creative in the way they approached Boaz. They did not rush into anything, they quietly observed and eventually Naomi came up with a plan. They charted a new course.

Boaz was a very wealthy man. I am positive that there were a number of young ladies who had their eyes on him. How was Ruth able to get his attention? She had to be creative in the way she handled things. Naomi knew that things had to be done differently.

Think about a time you experienced a service that stood out, maybe at a store, a restaurant or an office. What made the service stand out is most likely the "extra" in the way it was done. The person providing the service went above and beyond their call of duty. It could even be that the service was rendered uniquely or in a way that you have never experienced before.

That kind of service will stand out. It will make you want to share the information with your friends and family. It will make you want to come back to experience it again. And as a result, it will bring the service provider more growth and success in their business. All of this is the result of the ripple effect that accompanies creativity.

Creativity allows you to use your imagination and implement something in a way that may not have been done before. Your imagination is a powerful tool. Simply put, imagination means image formation.

What do you see? What things do you picture in your imagination? The image you form in your mind is the result you will get tomorrow. To achieve success, you must picture success.

When your imagination is at work, you are meditating. Meditating means to focus, or think deeply about a certain issue. Most people say that they do not know how to meditate, but the same people know how to worry. If you worry, you can definitely meditate. Worrying is paying attention, overthinking and pondering over a negative outcome of a certain circumstance.

It is wiser to spend your time meditating or using your imagination for your good. You can meditate on the positive outcome of scenarios. You can use your imagination to get answers for difficult situations. The bible tells us the connection between meditation and success in various books.

Study this Book of Instruction continually. Meditate on it day and night so you will be sure to obey everything written in it. Only then will you prosper and succeed in all you do.

Joshua 1:8

But they delight in the law of the LORD, meditating on it day and night. They are like trees planted along the riverbank, bearing fruit each season. Their leaves never wither, and they prosper in all they do.

Psalms 1:2-3

God has already given us the keys to our success. He has given us principles. Meditation is one of them. When we meditate on God's word, He will give us the answers to our questions. He will give us strategies to take our brands and businesses to the next level. Most people are stuck because they do not take the time to pause and reflect. They don't take time out to think. They do not take time to meditate.

Some cultures and families even discourage their young ones from being deep in thought. As a young man, growing up in Africa, I remember being questioned countless times for being deep in thought. "What are you thinking about? You are too young to be thinking so much. You do not have any children to think about." These are some of the statements I would hear. Thinking was only accepted if you had children to feed or responsibilities to take care of. These comments were definitely not intentional. Our parents did the best they knew how to, they just could not teach us what they did not know.

We know better now. The Bible mentions meditation as one of the principles of success. You have to use your mind to create the future you want to see. Your mind is a very powerful tool. That is why the Bible also advises us to guard our hearts and minds. What you expose your mind to will determine the image you form which will in turn determine the results you receive.

ARE MY GATES GUARDED?

Gates, in this context, are the entry or exit point of your mind. We already know that our creativity starts in the mind and is established by meditation and imagination. The mind is where all the great ideas begin. So wisdom will tell you that it is important to be aware of the things you allow to take residence in your mind.

The gates that you have are your eyes, your ears, and your mouth. When you go online to look for information to build your brand or business, you will watch videos, read articles, listen to podcasts and the likes. The eye and ear gates are the entry points to these information. The same gates are what we use when we are networking, having conversations and speaking to people one on one.

These gates are very important. If you hear or see the wrong thing and apply it to your business, then your business will be impacted negatively. This is why you must be protective of your gates.

What information do you allow through your gates? What are you watching? What are you listening to? Is it beneficial to you? Does it build you up or tear you down? Do you feel empowered or drained after you hear it? What images are formed in your mind based on the things that you allow through your gates?

When God wants to take you to the next level, he exposes you to something greater than what you have experienced prior to that time.. He allows you to see it or hear it and something changes in you. With such encounters, you would not want to go back to life and business as usual. In the same way, the enemy can also expose you to negative influences and if you are not careful to guard and protect your gates, this negativity will take residence in your mind and eventually be the picture that you have in your imagination. Of course, that will not lead you to success.

Your mouth gate is also very critical. It allows you to share information. If you are not wise and do not know how to guard this gate, it may land you in trouble. Many people have lost their money, their businesses and even their ideas because they shared it prematurely. They shared too much too soon, or they shared it with the wrong group of people.

Set a guard, O Lord, over my mouth; keep watch over the door of my lips [to keep me from speaking thoughtlessly]

Psalms 141:3

It is wise to guard your gates. Protect your anointing like you would the apple of your eye. Pray and ask God to teach you how to do this. But also take the necessary steps that you already know. Get rid of every negative influence. Be mindful of the environment you are in, the things that you watch, the information you hear and even what you say.

6

COURAGE

Imagine moving to a foreign country where everything is different from where you grew up. Different language, culture, traditions, and generally a different way of life. Not only is everything different, but you also have to fend for yourself. Imagine how challenging it may be to adjust and find your place in this new society.

For some, it is scary to even think of subjecting themselves to such a predicament. But in Ruth's case, she chose to go this route regardless of the looming uncertainties. When reading her story, it's so easy to assume she went through with this decision so effortlessly that we fail to put ourselves in her shoes and imagine all the odds she was truly up against.

Ruth was a foreigner in Israel, she could not speak the language and did not fully comprehend the culture and lifestyle of her new home. So you can imagine how she must have felt when she went to harvest in Boaz's field; she probably had an accent and was not fluent in her speaking. But that did not stop her from going after what she was looking for. She was still able to go boldly to the workers and request to harvest with them.

She did not disqualify herself because she was different from the natives. She did not talk herself out of leaving her house because she did not want to be judged. She did not put any limits on herself. Ruth was courageous.

Being courageous does not mean that you do not feel fear, rather it means that you step out anyway in spite of the fear. Being courageous means confronting your fear head on. It means you are doing it afraid.

The Bible is full of stories of courageous people. Young David fought Goliath, Moses led the Israelites out of Egypt even though he was afraid, Joshua and Caleb believed they could conquer the giants even when the majority did not agree with them. I could go on and on.

What are you doing to face your fears?

What are you holding off on because of your fears?

"Be strong and of good courage; do not fear nor be afraid of them; for the Lord your God, He is the One who goes with you. He will not leave you nor forsake you."

Deuteronomy 31:6

God has promised to be with you in every situation.

In his book, Think and Grow Rich, Napoleon Hill said, "There are no limitations to the mind except those that we acknowledge". The mind is a very powerful tool. What you believe and meditate on in your mind, will eventually become what manifests in your life.

COURAGE VS CONFIDENCE

Most people use these two words interchangeably even though they are different concepts. As mentioned above, courage is acting in spite of fear. Confidence on the other hand is the internal belief or certainty that one has of their ability.

Courage is daring. It is going against the external and internal forces that are a source of fear. It is stepping out in spite of the uncertainty. Confidence, on the other hand, is the belief that you have in yourself or your ability. Confidence knows how something works.

Usually, we spend a lot of time trying to build our confidence or waiting until we are confident before we begin something. We wait for confidence before we take action. I would like to propose that what you need is not confidence but courage. Courage is what allows you to start.

There is always a lot of uncertainty accompanying a new undertaking. What if it fails? What if we can't sustain it? What will people think? How will it do in the market? These are only a few of the questions that people tend to ask themselves. There is always uncertainty about the outcome or the response of others. In these moments of uncertainty, confidence is not what you need to take the first step. You will need courage.

Courage is what will help you take that first step to pursue what you want regardless of the uncertainty. Courage is what will help you attempt something that you have never tried before. Courage is what will help you to stand before strangers and share your product or service even though you are afraid that they may reject you. Courage is what you need to begin.

As mentioned before, confidence comes with a certainty. One is usually more confident doing something that they have done before and know its outcome. Confidence comes with practice. Confidence comes with trying, failing and trying again until you achieve the desired results. Confidence comes with testing and proving. Confidence is built over time as one becomes more familiar with their processes and their product. Confidence comes when you hone your skills over time with much practice.

Do not delay pursuing your God - given idea because you are waiting to be confident. Courage is all you need to begin.

WHAT ABOUT CONFIDENCE?

Does this mean that confidence is pointless? Not at all. Confidence is equally important, and it has its place.

Therefore do not cast away your confidence, which has a great reward. For you have need of endurance, so that after you have done the will of God, you may receive the promise.

Hebrews 10:35 - 36

As children of God, we are to be confident in the God that we serve. We are to be confident in His word and in His promises. The bible even tells us that we should approach God with confidence and boldness, believing that He is faithful to do what He said He will do.

There are two types of confidence:

Confidence in the flesh: this is the confidence in your human knowledge and understanding. It is the confidence that we have in man. This confidence is limited. Sometimes we operate in this and we think it is faith. The confidence that you place on man will usually fail.

Confidence in God: this is the ultimate confidence. Do not lose the confidence that you have in God. We know we can trust in Him because we have seen His track record. He told us to taste and see that He is good (Psalm 34:8), and any believer can attest that He surely is good. We have learnt to have confidence in Him because we have seen time and time again that He can be trusted to fulfil everything He said He would.

One of the ways one can lose their confidence in God is when there is sin. Sin is a confidence killer. Sin erodes confidence. When God gives you a word and you fail to obey it, you lose confidence to come back to him. The absence of confidence is usually the presence of condemnation.

Do your very best to not lose the confidence that you have in God. Be obedient to what He has asked you to do. Keep far away from sin and when you do fall, be sure to repent and ask for grace not to go back to it. Do your best to not have any unconfessed sin in your life. Do not allow the enemy or any circumstance destroy the confidence you have in God.

7

CHARISMA

The word charisma is from the Greek word "charis", which means gift. Like I mentioned previously, each one of us has a gift inside us. God has placed something special and unique in you that is needed in your generation. The Bible says in Proverbs 18:16 that the gift of a man makes room for him and ushers him into the presence of the great.

Everyone has a gift, what makes you become relevant is how you carry yourself. The younger generation has coined the word "swag". Your gift has to be embodied in swag and surprisingly, each of us already have that swag inbuilt in us. God created us with the inbuilt ability to be able to display our product on the shelf of destiny.

We have millions of information that go through our brain each day. Scientists have told us that there are 3 things that the brain takes notice of immediately: something that is unique, something that is valuable and something that is dangerous. In this current world filled with so much information, what will make you stand out is your uniqueness.

Your charisma has nothing to do with what you carry, what you carry is sure and secure. Rather, your charisma has to do with how you display what you carry. In order to stand out, you need to ask yourself the following questions:

- Who am I?
- What gift do I carry?
- What product do I have to offer?
- Who do I need to reach?
- Where do I need to reach them?
- How do I need to reach them?

- ❖ What is my success strategy? What does success mean to you?

If you are true to yourself while answering these questions, you will be able to evolve and the gift in you will be displayed.

Displaying your uniqueness is first an inside work. The beauty on the inside is what can be displayed on the outside. Whatever you carry inside you is what will pour out of you. Before you learn any practical skills on how to display your product or how to be charismatic, it is important that you take some time to deal with the things in your heart that could be a hindrance to you.

When you look at Ruth, she had gone through a lot of painful situations. She had lost her spouse and her in-laws, and lastly she lost her family of origin as she left Moab. In chapter 2, we see Ruth settling in and going to work in the fields. She gleaned there all through the harvest season to early summer (Ruth 2:23). Naomi already knew that Boaz was eligible to marry Ruth, but she did not bring it up until later in Chapter 3.

I believe that Naomi knew that Ruth needed some time to heal. She needed time to mourn and grieve her losses and also time to get acclimatised to her new life in Bethlehem. She did not rush the process.

Most times we need not rush into anything until we have dealt with the issues in our hearts. The pain that we feel, the losses that we have experienced and even pain caused by people who have hurt us. If we are not careful, we will bleed onto others and that is what will be displayed on the shelves of our destinies.

We all know or have heard of people who are angry and bitter because of the negative experiences of their lives. Whether children who were abused or adults who were wrongly accused, many people are hurting and angry at the world. Even though it was not of their doing, their healing is their responsibility.

Like Ruth, time for healing is needed and necessary before you can move on to the next phase of your life. Ruth did not allow where she came from to determine where she is going. Her background did not determine her destiny. She was able to display her uniqueness even when she was gleaning in Boaz's farm.

When Naomi saw that she was ready, she spoke to her about Boaz. In chapter 3:3, Naomi advises Ruth to "... take a bath and put on perfume and dress in your nicest clothes..." this signifies the outward presentation of the inward work that Ruth had done. It was now time to take off her widow's garments and move to the next level that God had prepared for her.

In the journey of rebranding yourself and displaying your product, do not neglect to create the inward beauty that will naturally pour out on the outside. Then, and only then is it a great time to learn the skill of being charismatic.

INFLUENCE AND AFFABILITY

When you walk into a room or have to stand before an audience, there are two things that you will want to portray. The first one is confidence; we want to appear calm, collected and ready to take on anything. The second one is charisma - we want to exude an irresistible charm. While confidence is more of an internal belief, charisma is a skill that can be learned and eventually mastered.

A study done by the University of Toronto researchers found that charisma consists of a blend of affability and influence. A charismatic person is pleasant and approachable, and at the same time has leadership abilities and a certain aura of strength.

A charismatic person has the ability to instil confidence in others, negotiate, persuade and convince others to follow them. As a brand, charisma is a necessary skill that you need to learn in order to be successful. Whether a business owner or an individual, charisma will open doors for you and get you into rooms you could not have imagined.

You have probably met a charismatic person, admired their charisma and assumed that they were born that way. Don't count yourself out just yet, charisma is a skill that can be learned and developed. Regardless of your personality type, it is quite possible to become charismatic.

THE SKILL OF CHARISMA

1. **Master the art of being present:**

Charismatic people are likeable people. Part of being likeable is being fully engaged in conversation or being fully present in what you are doing. Do not be that person that pulls out their phone in the middle of a conversation. Do not be the person who zones out when others are speaking, or only wants to speak about themselves.

Learn to be present in any activity. Listen with intent. This makes people feel valued and when you make them feel that way, they will want to be around you.

2. **Bring your power**

Portraying power is not a show of strength but it has everything to do with your body language. Your body language is a powerful tool during any conversation. Coupled with speaking, body language is what makes for effective communication. It does not matter what you say with your mouth, if your body language doesn't match it then there is an inconsistency in your communication that makes it difficult for others to believe you.

There are many resources that can help with body language techniques but these three quick tips can help you make a good first impression - have an open posture and relaxed posture, give firm handshakes and maintain eye contact. In a nutshell, a practical way to improve your body language is to visualise a triumphant situation and bring that body language to your conversations.

3. **Giving is better than receiving**

No one wants to hang around anyone that is always taking from them. A charismatic individual is a giving individual. Approaching people only when you want something from them will definitely lead to people avoiding you. When giving, it is important that you do not have ulterior motives. Let everything be an overflow of your character.

A giver provides a helping hand, a listening ear or even a smile during a busy day. All these will be appreciated when done with genuine intention. Develop the habit of being a giver, not because you are expecting something in return but because you are a generous individual.

There are countless other skills that can be learned with regard to being charismatic. Every day is an opportunity to be better. Prioritise your inward healing and it will naturally flow out of you. How your gift is displayed to the world will determine the audience that you attract. As a brand or business owner you know that marketing plays a huge role in bringing awareness to your brand or product. Your charisma is part of your marketing strategy. Master the art of being charismatic and you will definitely be ahead of the curve.

8

Crest

You have done the work. Your brand is making waves and you are seeing the result of all the work you have put in. You are finally at the very top. Your peers look up to you, they are all trying to learn from you. You stand before kings and prominent people. You have made it to the crest.

First of all, I want to congratulate you for working so hard on your brand and achieving your goals. It is amazing what you can achieve by being focused and putting in the work. Looking back, I am sure you have made many mistakes and have learned many lessons as a result of those mistakes. You have d charted paths that you probably never thought possible. You must be proud of all the amazing work you have done, and that is great.

Being at the top is usually a very coveted position. Many people are longing to be at the height of success in their field. Every day, there are a multitude of people online searching on how to be successful. Some people go to extreme measures just so they can get to the level of success that they desire.

As much as success is desired, there are very few resources that teach on how to handle success. Too often, we hear stories of successful people who have acted in a way that has caused them to lose their position. We hear of many who have fallen from their thrones as a result of not knowing how to handle the responsibilities that come with their position. It has been said that it is easier to handle failure than it is to handle success.

There are even those who had slacked off after getting to the crest, and as a result, they became replaced and lost their position of influence. A good example is the rise of technology and how it affects brick and mortar stores.

Everything can be found online now. When this trend first started, those who jumped on it made headway in this market. But those who delayed suffered a major decline to their sales as the years progressed. We see a number of major companies shut down each year. In order to keep up, you must be able to adapt to the changes.

MISTAKES PEOPLE MAKE WHEN THEY ARE AT THE TOP.

1. **Moral failure:**

Moral failure simply means deliberately doing something you know you should not be doing or vice versa. Many businesses have fallen because of this.. This calls to mind an old tale about a man and his son.This man sold fried fish, had loyal customers and was making a decent living. Daily, his business grew steadily. Eventually, his son joined the business after completing his university education. The son advised his father to consider making more money by cutting down cost. One of the strategies he suggested was buying fish in bulk instead of buying fresh fish daily as bulk purchase was cheaper than buying in smaller quantities.. He further advised him to reuse the oil he fried with, and buy packed seasoning instead of fresh seasoning. Again, his point was that fresh seasoning cost more. . The man obliged and proceeded to implement his son's advice.

Unfortunately, they soon started realising that the sales had dropped just as their costs had dropped as well. This continued until finally, a loyal customer complained that the quality of the fish was no longer as good as it used to be.. He said that a lot of people had been making the same complaint and were considering taking their patronage elsewhere. .This loyal customer also opened up to say that he was considering looking for another fried fish vendor. That was when it dawned on them, that the quality of their product was what attracted the customers in the first place.

In the course of the pursuit of success, do not get greedy that all you care about is making a quick buck. Greed causes people to lose their morals. This is what makes trusted accountants steal from their employers, this is what makes a shop owner have dishonest scales to cheat their clients. Be careful that you do not lose your morals all in the name of being successful. Remember that the world can forgive character failure but will not easily forgive moral failure.

2. Arrogance

Arrogant people are usually people who act like they are more important or superior to others. A big mistake that one can make is to be arrogant. Most people become arrogant after doing or achieving something great and worthy of note.

Everyone loves a good underdog story; you start at the bottom and work hard all the way to your crest. You become celebrated and a prominent member of the community. Now, wisdom tells you to remain humble but sometimes, one might not heed the voice of wisdom.

Arrogance comes along when one starts believing that they are where they are by their own strength. At this point, their self-worth is highly stimulated to the point where it is easy for them to look down on others who seem to be "lagging behind". Arrogance can also be caused by a deep sense of insecurity or low self-esteem. Most people suffer from imposter syndrome, and so they tend to use arrogance to cover up their insecurities.

For by the grace (unmerited favour of God) given to me I warn everyone among you not to estimate and think of himself more highly than he ought [not to have an exaggerated opinion of his own importance], but to rate his ability with sober judgment, each according to the degree of faith apportioned by God to him.

Romans 12:3

At your highest, do not forget where you came from. Do not forget the people who supported your journey to the top. No one makes it on their own. There is always a group of people who have supported you in one way or the other. There are always people who believed in you, showed you the ropes or gave you an opportunity that you would have otherwise not been able to receive. Honour those people, and more importantly, be there for others who are coming behind you.

3. Refusing to be corrected

Correction is painful and difficult to hear. It takes great humility to allow others to correct you. It is easy to get very defensive and feel some sort of resentment when one tries to correct us.

Apart from pride and having a bruised ego, there are two other things that make it very difficult to receive correction:

The method of delivery: the person doing the correction may be callous with their words. They may not say it very nicely. They may even expose you by saying it in a public place. This makes it very difficult to receive, even if what they are saying may be true.

The person giving the correction is flawed, younger or inexperienced: a good example is a parent being corrected by their child. Most times, it is awkward to receive criticism from your child who you consider young and inexperienced. What they are saying may be true but because they are your children, you do not feel like they should be correcting you. This is also true for when older people correct the young ones. Usually, young people feel like the older generation "do not understand" because things are different now than they were during the old times.

People who accept discipline are on the pathway to life, but those who ignore correction will go astray.

Proverbs 10:17

You will need to be willing to receive correction from others no matter how painful it may be. Always examine yourself before you reject and classify the people correcting you as "haters".

A few practical ways that may help on how to respond to correction:

Not being defensive: let defensiveness not be your first response. Receive it first then set some time aside to ponder over it.

With a grace-filled attitude: always have a gracious response. If you do not think you will be able to say anything nice without reacting defensively, it is better to be silent until you have calmed down or have taken time to think about what was said.

Self-evaluation or examination: not all criticism may be helpful for you. Not every advice is one that you should follow. Take some time to examine and evaluate yourself based on what was brought to your attention. Be honest with yourself.

Pray about it: this may seem cliché but it is vital that you bring everything to the Lord in prayer. Ask Him to show you your heart, ask Him to show you where you have gone wrong. You should even let Him know how this correction has made you feel. You will definitely find comfort in the Holy Spirit and He will lead you into all truth. God will give you direction on what to do, how to do it and the grace to do it.

Have some action steps: when you finally have things in perspective, prepare some action steps on how you are going to improve or do better based on the correction that has been given to you. Set some realistic goals. Also, give yourself grace. Remember that change takes time. Rome was not built in a day.

He cuts off every branch in me that bears no fruit, while every branch that does bear fruit he prunes so that it will be even more fruitful.

John 15:2

As painful as it is to receive correction, do not forget that often, the people who correct you want to see you win. They want to see you at your best. They are not correcting you just to hurt your feelings. Everyone has a blind spot, sometimes it takes others to point out something that is wrong before you realise that it is wrong. Like in John 15:2, pruning is painful, but it makes you become more fruitful. Be open and receptive to correction, and you will see even greater results.

4. Settling for the current level

When people feel that they have arrived, they stop doing what they did to get to their current level. You can and should still decide to go higher than where you are.

There is always more ahead. Do not settle for where you are no matter how good it seems to be.

Usain Bolt, a retired sprinter and a 9 time Olympic gold medallist, decided to pursue his dream of becoming a professional football player. This may sound surprising, considering all that he has achieved in his career. Bolt is a great example of one who does not settle because he is at the top. He knew that there was always more to achieve, and he was willing to work hard to achieve it.

From his story, we can learn that there is always a higher level. We do not need to settle where others are settling. We do not need to subscribe to the idea of stopping when the applause is the loudest. There is always more.

Many high achievers have done and are still doing what Usain Bolt did. They are not settling for where they are. They are not dwelling on past glories, instead, they keep going after all the things that they are passionate about.

You do not necessarily have to do or be only one thing. God has made us so intricately complex that He has placed various gifts and desires in us. Being successful in one, does not limit the pursuit of other interests. Do not settle for the status quo. Do not put a muzzle on your potential. There is more to you than you think, therefore, do not be a hindrance to your growth. Make a decision to never live in mediocrity, instead, diligently work to maximise your potential and become everything that God has created you to be.

PREPARE TO BE EFFECTIVE AND MAKE AN IMPACT

As a trailblazer, you should expect to have those who look up to you. Whenever you are at the crest, you become a leader in your field. Many others will look up to you and your influence may become substantial. It is wise that you set the right example for others to follow.

Even though this sounds exciting, there is a responsibility that comes with influence. When you know that there are others following you without question, you should be intentional about the things you do so that you do not lead them astray. It is therefore important that you prepare yourself to be an effective leader and make a positive impact in your community.

You have probably heard of this age-long maxim that says, "You can't pour from an empty cup". Simply, this means that you cannot give what you do not have. Before you can help anyone else out, you need to be in a better place first. A few things that can help to build you up as a leader are:

1. **Set your goals:**

We have spoken extensively about setting goals in the second chapter of this book. Set goals that will inspire and motivate you to get things done. In Chapter 2, we discussed setting SMART goals. Just to recap, SMART goals are **s**pecific, **m**easurable, **a**ttainable, **r**ealistic and **t**ime-bound.

Another critical tip on goal setting is having your goals written down. There is something powerful about putting pen to paper and clearly stating your goal. A goal not written down is only a wish, so cultivate the habit of writing down your goals.

After writing it down, make an action plan and follow through. You cannot really achieve anything if you do not set implementation plans in place. Set yourself up for success ahead of time by proper planning and follow through.

2. Get a mentor

Pouring into others is great, but what is even greater is having others who pour into you. No one knows everything, and no man is an island. We all need each other in order to succeed. Mentors are a great resource; they afford you an opportunity to learn from those who have gone ahead of you, are more experienced and more knowledgeable.

A good mentor will test, stretch and motivate you to do and be better. Being a mentee means that you are a student and are also learning from someone. This is the relevant experience for when you mentor others, you will know what it's like to be a mentee. It is easier and more efficient to help someone when you have been in their shoes.

Other than that, mentorship helps us to not repeat mistakes. We will know what to do and what not to do by getting advice from our mentors because they have been there and are experienced. What may take you 10 years to achieve can be achieved in 5 years if you have a mentor to show you the way.

3. Read books

The average CEOs and executives read about 60 books a year. If the leaders and game changers of the world read that many books, it is clear that there is some value gleaned from this reading habit. Harry Truman said that leaders are readers. You cannot lead effectively if you do not read.

Books are a rich source of information, therefore, reading increases your knowledge. You learn various topics that you otherwise would not have learnt on your own. Apart from that, reading improves your brain, expands your vocabulary, develops critical thinking and even increases your emotional intelligence. These are all critical life skills that you need for success. Reading makes you a good communicator, and as a leader, being a good communicator is a necessary skill.

Cultivate the habit of reading books on various topics. You can start with smaller books or topics that you are very excited about. If you are among the people who do not like to sit down with a book, or are too busy to include reading in your schedule - technology has made everything easier for you today. There are many audio books available that you can listen to as you are commuting, taking a walk or running on the treadmill. There are no excuses to not be a reader anymore.

THE ULTIMATE GOAL

You are the light of the world. A town built on a hill cannot be hidden. 15 Neither do people light a lamp and put it under a bowl. Instead they put it on its stand, and it gives light to everyone in the house. 16 In the same way, let your light shine before others, that they may see your good deeds and glorify your Father in heaven.

Matthew 5: 14-16

As children of God, we are His representatives here on earth. He made us in His image and likeness, in other words, he has branded us as His children. The Bible says in Matthew 5 that when our light shines, others will see our good deeds and glorify God. So we know that ultimately, in everything we do, the goal is to give God all the glory. Our brand is not about us.

Everything we have learned and spoken about in this book would mean nothing if God is not glorified. I pray that the words you have read in this book will inspire you to be at your best because you know who you are representing here on earth. I pray that God will be glorified through your brand. I pray that this book has inspired you to put your best foot forward, as you go about being the light that you were called to be.